DEDICATION

To my niece, Naomi Eseosa Okungbowa, may you thrive in happiness and prosperity.

To my sister, Onovughode Oboh, thank you for always believing in me and for your unconditional support.

To my goddaughters, Amari Lakayla Simmons and Destini Lyniya Jones: Always remember that you are the future, and you can do anything to which you set your mind.

To my parents, thank you for creating the woman I have become today.

To my big blended family, thank you for giving me a place to belong.

To all the little boys and girls, keep dreaming, because you are magic.

A

A is for ASSETS

Assets always produce value,
and value is the true measure of success.

B

B is for BILLIONAIRE

There are 1,810 billionaires in the world,
and you can become one, too!

C

C is for CEO (Chief Operating Officer)

Mommy and Daddy are the CEOs of their companies,
and any moment now, you will be starting
your own company, too!

D

D is for DIVIDENDS

Daddy buys Mommy a diamond every time
he receives his dividends.

E

E is for EMPIRE

Mommy and Daddy created one, and
now it's up to you to continue their legacy.

F

F is for *FORBES* MAGAZINE

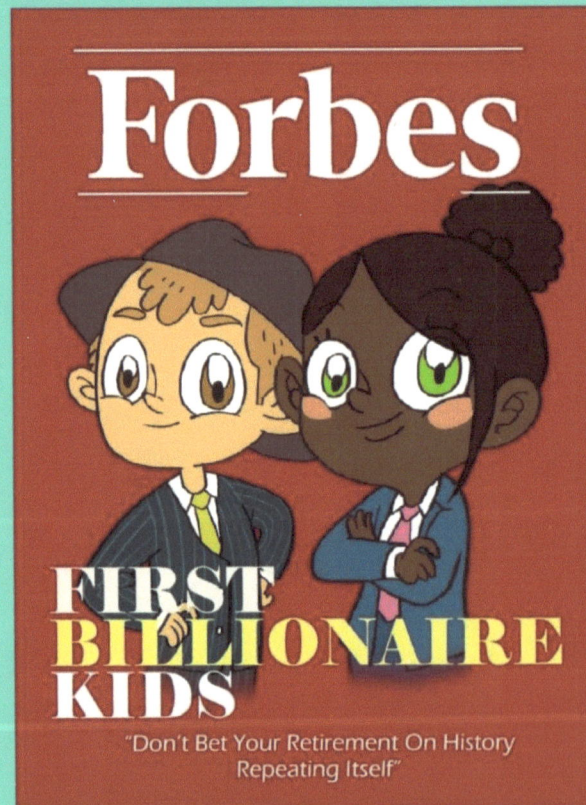

This is the only list on which you want to be included;
for once you've made it in there, you can make it anywhere!

G

G is for GUCCI

Daddy loves golfing at the country club
in his Gucci loafers.

H

H is for HELICOPTER

Mommy and Daddy always take the helicopter
from Manhattan to the Hamptons to avoid traffic.

I

I is for INVESTMENT

An investment grows over time, so invest in yourself
as much as you can. Just like your monetary investment,
you will also grow and accumulate value.

J

J is for JET

A private jet is the most luxurious and efficient way
to travel. Daddy can attend business meetings
in several countries in one day!

K

K is for KINDNESS

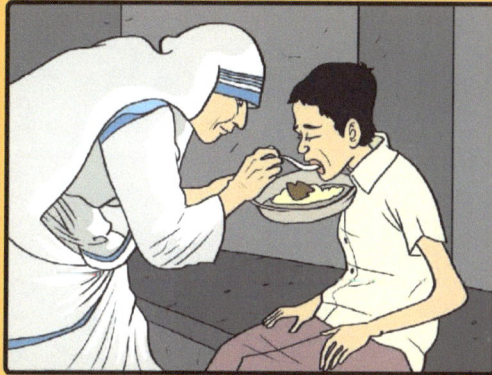

Kind people are the best kind of people. Greet everyone
you meet with a warm smile. Cultivating kindness
is a valuable part of the business of life.

L

L is for LOUIS VUITTON

With all the money Mommy gets from her rental properties, she can buy all the Louis Vuitton bags she wants! It is her favorite luggage when she travels.

M

M is for MANSION

With an east and west wing, there is plenty of room
to run around and play!

N

N is for NET WORTH

The higher your net worth, the more good you can do
in the world by helping others.

O

O is for OPERA

We should always support the arts, because it has the potential to teach powerful life lessons and spark creativity within us. Attending the opera allows people to experience art in its fullest form.

P

P is for PASSIVE INCOME

If you want to earn passive income and make money while you sleep, you need to invest time and money into making sure your business runs efficiently.

Q

Q is for QUESTION

It is very important that you think for yourself.
Therefore, you must read and question everything
you read. Question everything you see and hear,
and you might end up being the voice of your peers.

R

R is for RESIDUALS

Mommy bought her Rolls Royce with
the residuals from her book deal.

S

S is for ST. TROPEZ

The family summer vacations are always spent in
the south of France in St. Tropez. This gives you a chance
to practice your French. After all, you are multilingual.

T

T is for TRAVEL

Travel is one of the best forms of education. You can gain new experiences, make new friends, and learn about different cultures just by visiting a new country.

U

U is for UNIQUE

You are special and truly one of a kind.
Stay true to who you are, and embrace your
uniqueness, for that is the key to happiness.

V

V is for VERSACE

Mommy always wears her Versace dress when
she goes dancing with Daddy.

W

W is for WEALTH

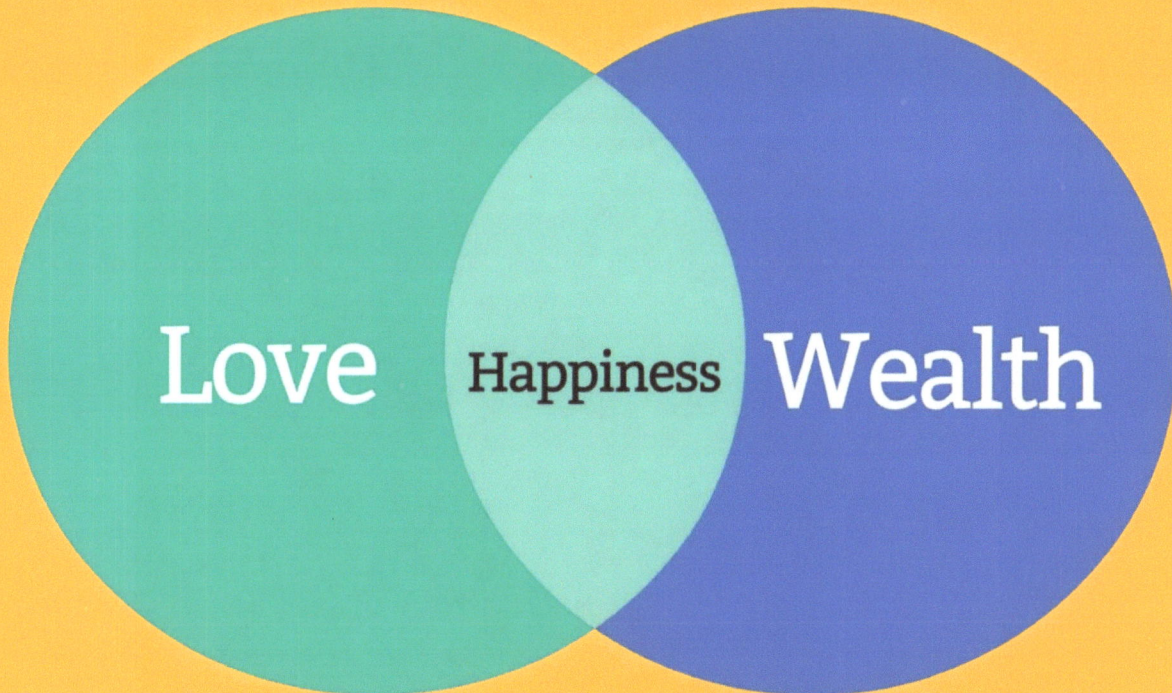

Love Happiness Wealth

True wealth is measured not only by how much cash and assets you have but also by how much love and happiness you have in your life.

X

X is for XI

This is the fourteenth letter of the Greek alphabet.
The ancient Greeks have greatly influenced and contributed
to today's culture, literature, architecture, music, technology,
food, and sports. It is always important to know history.

Y

Y is for YACHT

Sunbathing on a yacht in the Caribbean is always
a relaxing way to spend the weekend.

Z

Z is for ZEAL

Make sure you do everything with zeal.
When you are passionate about your goals,
you will be successful beyond your wildest dreams.

www.ingramcontent.com/pod-product-compliance
Lightning Source LLC
Chambersburg PA
CBHW041240040426

42445CB00004B/93